Blastoff! Discovery launches a new mission: reading to learn. Filled with facts and features, each book offers you an exciting new world to explore!

This is not an official DreamWorks book. It is not approved by or connected with DreamWorks.

This edition first published in 2025 by Bellwether Media, Inc.

No part of this publication may be reproduced in whole or in part without written permission of the publisher.
For information regarding permission, write to Bellwether Media, Inc., Attention: Permissions Department,
6012 Blue Circle Drive, Minnetonka, MN 55343.

Library of Congress Cataloging-in-Publication Data

LC record for DreamWorks available at: https://lccn.loc.gov/2024021926

Text copyright © 2025 by Bellwether Media, Inc. BLASTOFF! DISCOVERY and associated logos are trademarks and/or registered trademarks of Bellwether Media, Inc. Bellwether Media is a division of Chrysalis Education Group.

Editor: Betsy Rathburn   Series Designer: Andrea Schneider   Book Designer: Josh Brink

Printed in the United States of America, North Mankato, MN.

TABLE OF CONTENTS

FAMILY MOVIE NIGHT	4
THE DREAM BEGINS	6
MORE HITS	20
HELPING HANDS	26
FAN FUN	28
GLOSSARY	30
TO LEARN MORE	31
INDEX	32

FAMILY MOVIE NIGHT

It is Friday night. A family settles in to watch a DreamWorks movie. The popcorn is popped. The lights are dim. Now, the family needs to decide which movie to watch. The youngest family member suggests *Trolls*. But her older brother wants to watch *How to Train Your Dragon*. The kids' dad wants to watch *Wallace & Gromit: The Curse of the Were-Rabbit*. Their mom suggests a classic like *Shrek*!

Eventually, the family decides on a DreamWorks film none of them has seen. They choose *Kung Fu Panda 4*. The whole family loves it!

KUNG FU PANDA 4

HOW TO TRAIN YOUR DRAGON

THE DREAM BEGINS

DREAMWORKS HEADQUARTERS
GLENDALE, CALIFORNIA

TROLLS WORLD TOUR

DreamWorks **Animation** is an entertainment company. Its **headquarters** is in Glendale, California. DreamWorks is known for its animated films, such as the Trolls and Shrek **franchises**. It also makes animated TV shows. *Gabby's Dollhouse* and *The Boss Baby: Back in Business* are popular DreamWorks TV series. Both shows can be streamed online.

There are many other ways for fans to enjoy DreamWorks. Fans enjoy collecting toys based on their favorite characters and playing video games based on their favorite movies. In the future, they may be able to visit DreamWorks theme parks!

DREAMWORKS HEADQUARTERS

GLENDALE, CALIFORNIA

DreamWorks was **founded** as DreamWorks SKG on October 12, 1994. Steven Spielberg, Jeffrey Katzenberg, and David Geffen started the company. *SKG* stood for the founders' last names. All three men had experience in the film **industry**.

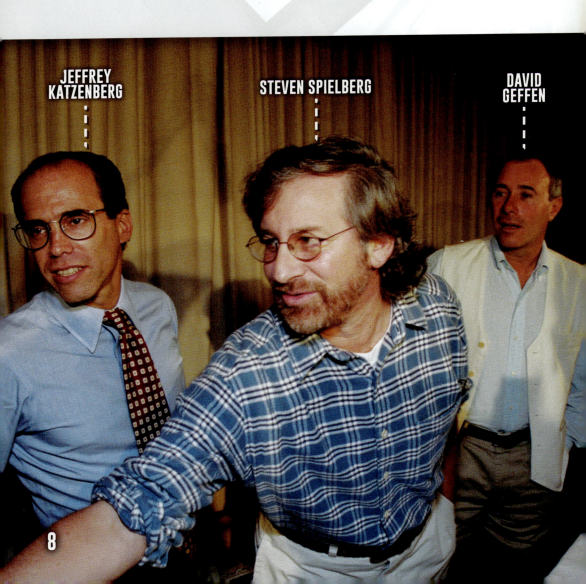

JEFFREY KATZENBERG STEVEN SPIELBERG DAVID GEFFEN

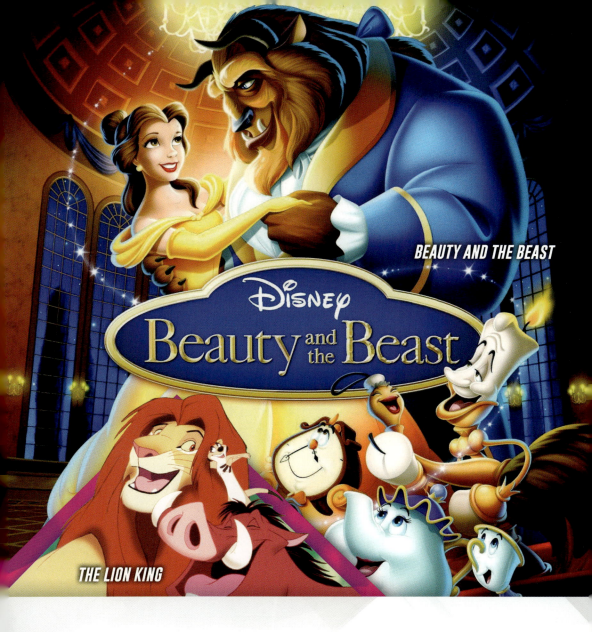

BEAUTY AND THE BEAST

THE LION KING

Jeffrey had spent 10 years working at Disney. There, he led the creation of many of Disney's animated films, including *The Little Mermaid*, *The Lion King*, and *Beauty and the Beast*. Because of Jeffrey's experience, he became the leader of DreamWorks's animation **division**. He and his partners hoped their new **studio** could compete with Disney.

Jeffrey focused on DreamWorks's animated films. Meanwhile, the company also made **live-action** films. Many were successful. Some even won major awards!

MUSIC, TOO!

DreamWorks Records launched in 1996. It featured popular artists such as Toby Keith and Nelly Furtado. In 2003, DreamWorks agreed to sell its record label for around $100 million!

JEFFREY KATZENBERG

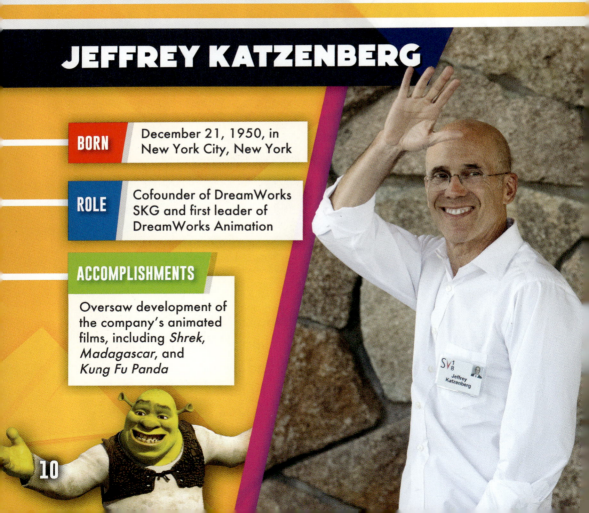

BORN: December 21, 1950, in New York City, New York

ROLE: Cofounder of DreamWorks SKG and first leader of DreamWorks Animation

ACCOMPLISHMENTS: Oversaw development of the company's animated films, including *Shrek*, *Madagascar*, and *Kung Fu Panda*

10

Most of the company's live-action films were meant for adults. But in 1997, the company released *Mouse Hunt*. This movie was made for both kids and adults. In it, two brothers compete against a clever mouse. **Critics** gave the film mixed reviews. But it did well at the **box office**, earning more than $120 million worldwide!

11

In 1998, DreamWorks finally released its first two animated films. They were *The Prince of Egypt* and *Antz*. Critics liked both films. *The Prince of Egypt* earned more than $218 million. It was the most successful non-Disney animated movie that year.

ANTZ

A BUG'S LIFE

Antz earned more than $170 million. But it faced competition from Disney. Disney's *A Bug's Life* was a similar insect movie released the same year. It earned more than $360 million. If DreamWorks wanted to compete with Disney, it needed a big hit.

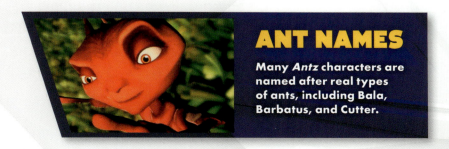

ANT NAMES

Many *Antz* characters are named after real types of ants, including Bala, Barbatus, and Cutter.

13

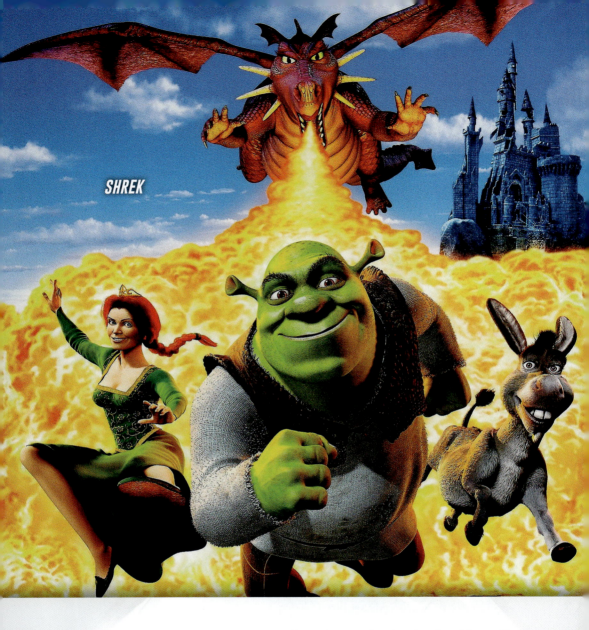

SHREK

In May 2001, DreamWorks released *Shrek*. The film tells the story of a grumpy green ogre. It was an instant hit. It earned more than $42 million in its first weekend. It went on to earn more than $480 million worldwide! Fans could not get enough of Shrek and its characters. They collected toys, bought special green foods, and more!

The movie proved DreamWorks could compete with Disney. For the first time ever, the summer's most popular animated movie was not a Disney film. *Shrek* even won the first-ever **Academy Award** for Best Animated Feature!

BOOK FIRST
The movie *Shrek* is based on a book called *Shrek!* by William Steig. Soon after it was released in 1990, Steven Spielberg planned to make it into a movie.

SHREK PRODUCER HOLDING ACADEMY AWARD

In 2004, DreamWorks SKG decided to break off the animation part of its business. DreamWorks Animation was now its own company. Jeffrey led the new business. That same year, DreamWorks Animation released two films. A *Shrek* **sequel** called *Shrek 2* came out in May. *Shark Tale* came out in October.

EARLY DREAMWORKS ANIMATED MOVIES

THE PRINCE OF EGYPT
YEAR 1998
BOX OFFICE SALES $218,613,188

CHICKEN RUN
YEAR 2000
BOX OFFICE SALES $224,888,359

SHREK
YEAR 2001
BOX OFFICE SALES $488,628,188

SHARK TALE
YEAR 2004
BOX OFFICE SALES $374,583,879

SHREK 2
YEAR 2004
BOX OFFICE SALES $932,395,557

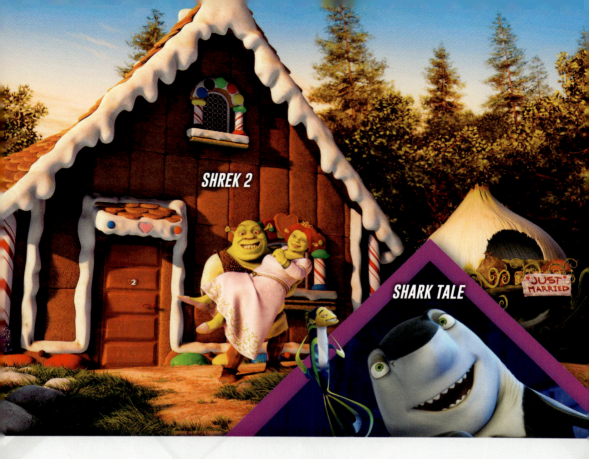

SHREK 2

SHARK TALE

Many critics gave *Shark Tale* negative reviews. But the film still earned more than $370 million. *Shrek 2* was more successful. It earned more than $930 million, nearly twice as much as the original movie. *Shrek 2* would become the company's highest-earning animated movie of all time!

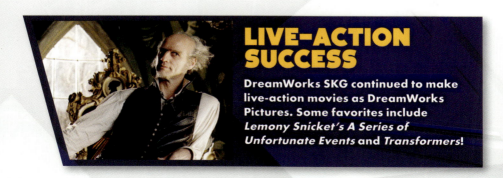

LIVE-ACTION SUCCESS

DreamWorks SKG continued to make live-action movies as DreamWorks Pictures. Some favorites include *Lemony Snicket's A Series of Unfortunate Events* and *Transformers*!

During this time, DreamWorks was shifting from hand-drawn animation to computer animation. Starting with *Shrek 2*, all DreamWorks movies were made with computer animation. The movie's popularity showed that this could be successful.

Shrek 2 also proved that DreamWorks could build a successful franchise. The company looked for ways to expand other stand-alone films into series. In 2005, DreamWorks had another hit with the release of *Madagascar*. It led to several **spin-offs** and sequels. There were even Madagascar TV shows. DreamWorks Animation was on a roll!

MADAGASCAR

DREAMWORKS TIMELINE

1994 — Steven Spielberg, Jeffrey Katzenberg, and David Geffen start DreamWorks SKG

2004 — DreamWorks Animation splits off from DreamWorks SKG

2016 — NBCUniversal buys DreamWorks

2024 — *Kung Fu Panda 4* is released

1998 — DreamWorks releases *Antz*

2005 — DreamWorks Animation releases *Madagascar*

2008 — *Kung Fu Panda* is released

2021 — *Gabby's Dollhouse* is released on Netflix

2001 — *Shrek* is released

SHREK 5

In 2023, DreamWorks announced a fifth Shrek film. Fans hope it will be released in 2025.

MORE HITS

KUNG FU PANDA

DreamWorks continued to churn out hits. In 2008, DreamWorks released *Kung Fu Panda*. This was the first film in the Kung Fu Panda series. The 2024 release of *Kung Fu Panda 4* grew the franchise's overall earnings to more than $2 billion!

In 2010, *How to Train Your Dragon* was released. *The Croods* came out in 2013. Sequels of each of these movies followed. Meanwhile, the company also brought some if its most popular characters to television. TV series starring characters from *Shrek, How to Train Your Dragon*, and other films were popular.

FAVORITE DREAMWORKS CHARACTERS

SHREK
First Appearance: *Shrek*

PUSS IN BOOTS
First Appearance: *Shrek 2*

TOOTHLESS
First Appearance: *How to Train Your Dragon*

POPPY
First Appearance: *Trolls*

OSCAR
First Appearance: *Shark Tale*

KING JULIEN
First Appearance: *Madagascar*

MARGIE COHN

By 2016, big changes were in store for DreamWorks Animation. NBCUniversal Studios bought the company for $3.8 billion. Soon after the sale, Jeffrey left the company. In time, Margie Cohn, who had led DreamWorks Animation Television, became president of the company.

In 2016, DreamWorks also released *Trolls*. The film was based on popular troll doll toys. *Trolls* released to mostly positive reviews and earned $347 million worldwide. The film featured the voices of well-known pop stars, including Justin Timberlake. It was the beginning of DreamWorks's next major franchise. Sequels followed in 2020 and 2023.

COOL CREATURES
The original troll doll toys were modeled after creatures from Scandinavian folklore!

JUSTIN TIMBERLAKE

TROLLS

DreamWorks found success with its franchises. But success is not always easy to find. The studio released a series of **flops** between 2019 and 2023. This included 2021's *Spirit Untamed*. Many fans liked the movie. But it was DreamWorks's lowest-earning movie of all time.

TODAY'S FAVORITES

Movie	Box Office Sales (in millions)
Spirit Untamed	$42 million
The Boss Baby: Family Business	$147 million
The Bad Guys	$250 million
Trolls Band Together	$209 million
Kung Fu Panda 4	$521 million

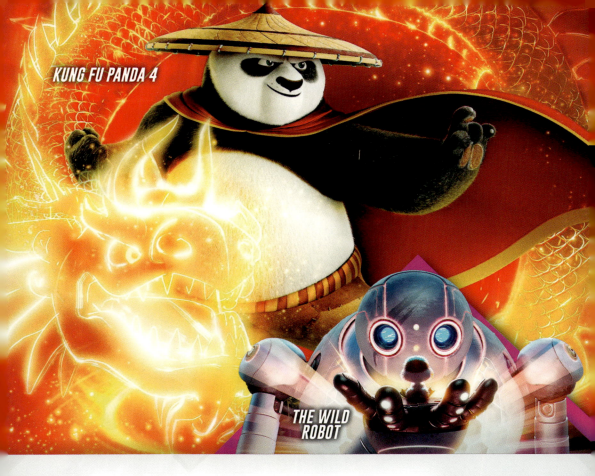

KUNG FU PANDA 4

THE WILD ROBOT

The company bounced back. In March 2024, DreamWorks released *Kung Fu Panda 4*. Many fans turned out to see the film. It earned more than $520 million worldwide! DreamWorks has many other projects planned. In 2023, the company announced it would release a movie called *The Wild Robot* in 2024. DreamWorks Animation always has exciting movies and TV shows in the works!

DOG MAN

Dog Man is a book series that started in 2016. In 2020, DreamWorks announced it would release a movie based on the books in 2025.

HELPING HANDS

2012 MOTION PICTURE & TELEVISION FUND EVENT

DreamWorks gives back to its community. In 2012, the founders of DreamWorks gave $90 million to the Motion Picture & Television Fund. This fund provides housing and health care to people who have worked in the film industry.

The company gives money to help people get enough food. In 2017, DreamWorks gave more than $20,000 and 38,000 food items to a **food bank** in California. In 2020, the DreamWorks movie *The Croods: A New Age* helped Feeding America food banks provide 1 million meals to families in need!

GIVING BACK

MORE THAN 38,000 FOOD ITEMS
GIVEN TO THE RESCUE MISSION ALLIANCE VALLEY FOOD BANK IN 2017

$90 MILLION
GIVEN BY DREAMWORKS'S FOUNDERS TO THE MOTION PICTURE & TELEVISION FUND IN 2012

1 MILLION MEALS
GIVEN TO FEEDING AMERICA AFTER THE RELEASE OF *THE CROODS: A NEW AGE* IN 2020

FAN FUN

2019 COMIC-CON CONVENTION

DreamWorks has found ways to bring its characters to life for its fans. It releases toys and video games based on popular DreamWorks films. Fans can attend **conventions** to learn about new films and celebrate old ones. DreamWorks Water Park is also fun for fans. They can splash, race down slides, and more.

28

Other events add even more fun. The Trolls LIVE! tour lets *Trolls* fans watch their favorite characters come to life with music, dancing, and fun! From 2014 to 2023, an annual Shrekfest was held in Wisconsin. It included Shrek-themed foods, costumes, and more. DreamWorks delights people of all ages!

DREAMWORKS WATER PARK

WHAT IT IS
An indoor water park with DreamWorks-themed slides, a large pool, costumed characters, and more

WHERE IT IS
East Rutherford, New Jersey

WHEN IT OPENED
October 2020

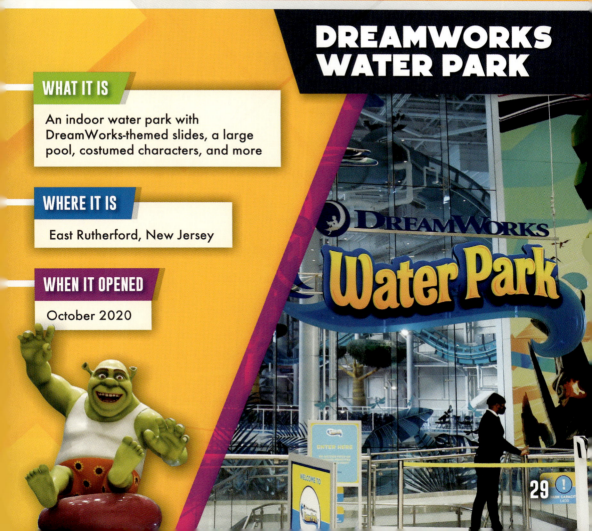

GLOSSARY

Academy Award—a yearly award presented for achievement in film; an Academy Award is also called an Oscar.

animation—a series of drawings that are shown quickly, one after the other, to give the appearance of movement

box office—a measure of ticket sales sold by a film or other performance

conventions—events where fans of a subject meet

critics—people who give opinions on movies and other entertainment

division—a group within a company

flops—films that are considered very unsuccessful or unprofitable

food bank—a place that gives food to people in need

founded—started or created

franchises—collections of books, movies, or other media that are related to one another

headquarters—a company's main office

industry—a group of businesses that provide a certain product

live-action—filmed using real actors

sequel—a movie that continues the story that started in a movie that came before it

spin-offs—movies, TV shows, or books that are based on another movie, TV show, or book

studio—a place where movies are filmed

TO LEARN MORE

AT THE LIBRARY

Barretta, Gene. *Starring Steven Spielberg: The Making of a Young Filmmaker*. New York, N.Y.: Little, Brown and Company, 2022.

Bolte, Mari. *Important Jobs on Movie Sets*. North Mankato, Minn.: Spark, 2023.

Green, Sara. *Disney*. Minneapolis, Minn.: Bellwether Media, 2023.

ON THE WEB

FACTSURFER

Factsurfer.com gives you a safe, fun way to find more information.

1. Go to www.factsurfer.com.
2. Enter "DreamWorks" into the search box and click 🔍.
3. Select your book cover to see a list of related content.

INDEX

animated movies, 5, 6, 9, 10, 12, 13, 14, 15, 16, 17, 18, 19, 20, 21, 23, 24, 25, 27
awards, 10, 15
characters, 7, 13, 14, 21, 28, 29
Cohn, Margie, 22
computer animation, 18
conventions, 28
Disney, 9, 12, 13, 15
DreamWorks Animation, 16, 18, 22, 25
DreamWorks Records, 10
DreamWorks Water Park, 28, 29
early DreamWorks animated movies, 16
fans, 7, 14, 19, 24, 25, 28, 29
Feeding America, 27
Geffen, David, 8
giving back, 27
Glendale, California, 6, 7
Katzenberg, Jeffrey, 8, 9, 10, 16, 22
Kung Fu Panda (franchise), 5, 20, 25
live-action movies, 10, 11, 17
Motion Picture & Television Fund, 26
name, 8
NBCUniversal Studios, 22
sales, 11, 12, 13, 14, 16, 17, 20, 23, 24, 25
sequels, 16, 17, 18, 20, 21, 23
Shrek (franchise), 5, 6, 14, 15, 16, 17, 18, 19, 21, 29
Shrekfest, 29
Spielberg, Steven, 8, 15
Timberlake, Justin, 23
timeline, 19
today's favorites, 24
Trolls (franchise), 5, 6, 23, 29
Trolls LIVE! tour, 29
TV shows, 6, 18, 21, 25

The images in this book are reproduced through the courtesy of: TCD/Prod.DB/ Alamy, front cover (hero Troll), pp. 6 (*Trolls World Tour*), 25 (*Kung Fu Panda 4*); Album/ Alamy, front cover (*How to Train Your Dragon 2*), pp. 9 (*The Lion King*) 13 (*A Bug's Life*), 17, 20 (*Kung Fu Panda*), 21 (Shrek, Puss In Boots), 24 (*The Bad Guys*); PictureLux/ Alamy, front cover (*Kung Fu Panda*), p. 15 (*Shrek*); Stefano Chiacchiarini '74/ Alamy, front cover (*Turbo* DVD); RGR Collection/ Alamy, front cover (*Madagascar*); Sarunyu L, front cover (*Trolls* poster); Jaguar PS, front cover (*Shrek*); Marko Aliaksandr, front cover (DreamWorks home page); Anton_Ivanov, front cover (Gingerbread Man); yackers1, p. 2 (movies); maxgarapu, pp. 3, 31; undefined undefined, pp. 4-5; FlixPix/ Alamy, p. 5 (*Kung Fu Panda 4*); Cinematic Collection/ Alamy, pp. 5 (*How to Train Your Dragon*), 13 (*Antz* bottom), 14, 16 (*Chicken Run*), 16 (*Shrek 2* movie case); Bloomberg/ Getty Images, p. 6 (DreamWorks headquarters); Ars1, p. 7 (Glendale, California); Steven D Starr/ Getty Images, p. 8; Maximum Film/ Alamy, pp. 9 (*Beauty and the Beast*), 10 (*Shrek*), 12, 17; Drew Angerer/ Getty Images, p. 10 (Jeffrey Katzenberg); Everett Collection/ Alamy, p. 11; Collection Christophel/ Alamy, pp. 13 (*Antz* top), 19 (*Shrek*), 24 (*The Boss Baby 2: Family Business*); DatBot/ Wikipedia, p. 15 (*Shrek!* book); Myung Jung Kim/ Alamy, p. 15 (Academy Award); Photo12/ Alamy, p. 17 (bottom); ABACAPRESS/ Alamy, p. 18; Wdwdbot/ Wikipedia, p. 19 (1999 entry); CNBC Europe promotional brochure, p. 19 (2016 entry); Entertainment Pictures/ Alamy, pp. 19 (bottom), 21 (Oscar), 23 (Justin Timberlake); TM & copyright ©20th Century Fox Film Corp./ Everett Collection, p. 21 (Toothless, Poppy); Entertainment Pictures/ Alamy, p. 21 (Oscar); DreamWorks/ Everett Collection, p. 21 (King Julien); Media Punch/ Alamy, p. 22; Amy Cicconi/ Alamy, p. 23 (top); Photo 12/ Alamy, p. 23 (*Trolls*); BFA/ Alamy, pp. 24 (*Spirit Untamed*), 25 (*The Wild Robot*); Stefano Chiacchiarini '74, p. 24 (*Trolls Band Together*); VisualArtStudio, p. 25 (*Dog Man*); Stefanie Keenan/ Getty Images, p. 26; Alucardion, p. 27 (top); ElenaR, p. 27 (bottom left); Prostock-studio, p. 27 (bottom right); Joe Scarnici/ Getty Images, p. 28; Adonis Page, p. 29.